Old CATHCART, LANGSIDE and MOUNT

by
Eric Eunson

Marchmont Terrace - Langside   GG1

These tenements in Marchmont Terrace date from the 1880s and were the first to be built in Battlefield, until then largely composed of detached villas. The street was renamed Grange Road, after Sir William Kirkcaldy of Grange, an estate near Kinghorn in Fife. He commanded the Regent Moray's cavalry at Langside and it was his leadership that took the battle, although he himself died in the fray.

© Eric Eunson 1999
First published in the United Kingdom, 1999,
Reprinted 2001
by Stenlake Publishing, 54-58 Mill Square, Catrine, Ayrshire. KA5 6RD
Telephone/Fax: 01290 551122
e-mail: sales@stenlake.co.uk website: www.stenlake.co.uk

ISBN 1 84033 093 7

THE PUBLISHERS REGRET THAT THEY CANNOT SUPPLY
COPIES OF ANY PICTURES FEATURED IN THIS BOOK.

FURTHER READING

The books listed below were used by the author during his research. None of them are available from Stenlake Publishing.
Those interested in finding out more are advised to contact their local bookshop or reference library.

Biggar, J.F., *The Battle of Langside*, 1568-1968
Doak, Young, *Glasgow at a Glance*, 1977
Glasgow Dist. Council, *Cathcart Heritage Trail*, 1990
Inglis, Simon, *The Football Grounds of Great Britain*, 1987
Marshall, Jean *Why Cathcart?*, 1975
Smart, Aileen, *Villages of Glasgow*, Volume 2, 1996
Williamson, E, Riches, A., *The Buildings of Scotland*, Glasgow, 1990
Worsdall, Frank, *The Glasgow Tenement*, 1979

Acknowledgements;
The author would like to thank Robert L. Grieves of Paisley for permission to use the pictures
on the front cover, inside front cover and pages 16, 30, 32.

INTRODUCTION

At the end of the eighteenth century the city of Glasgow had yet to cross the river Clyde. South of the river lay an entirely rural area, dotted with hamlets, steadings and country seats, and divided into ancient parishes. One of these was Cathcart, bounded on the north by Crossmyloof and Crosshill, on the west by Langside, Merrylee and Williamwood, on the south by Clarkston, and on the east by the estate of Aikenhead, now developed as King's Park. Cathcart lay within the county of Renfrewshire and its eastern edge formed part of the border with Lanarkshire.

Various derivations are suggested for the origin of the name Cathcart, the most popular being the Celtic "caer+cart", meaning "the fort by the stream". With this is advanced the notion that Cathcart may once have contained a fortress of great antiquity. However, the words "caer" and "cathair", meaning a village, are often confused by historians and it may be that the name means simply "village by a stream".

Cathcart Church is supposed to have been founded in the ninth century and was dedicated to St. Oswald, a king of Northumbria, who spent time at Iona and is said to have died in 642 A.D. in battle with Penda "the champion of paganism." An ancient holy well dedicated to St. Oswald was situated in the south east corner of Cathcart churchyard but was filled in in the late nineteenth century.

King David I (1124-1153) bestowed a vast estate on his steward Walter Fitzalan, which included "Passelet (Paisley), Renfrew, Polloc, Kerkert (Cathcart) and Eaglisham". Fitzalan in turn granted portions of these lands to various noblemen, among them Rainaldus, described variously as a Breton and a Dane at the Norman court, who was granted "Kerkert" and took his surname from the estate as was the custom at the time. He would have been obligated to erect a fortress on his land for the defence of the realm. This would almost certainly have been a motte and bailey, a defensive mound capped with a wooden fort surrounded by a palisade of stakes. This probably gave way to a small stone castle in the early thirteenth century. In the last quarter of the twelfth century Walter Fitzalan granted Cathcart Parish Church to the Priory, later Abbey, of Paisley, and they received its revenues until the the Reformation in 1560.

Rainaldus de Kerkert founded the family of Cathcart, whose bloodline continues uninterrupted to this day, although the family have had no involvement with the area since the 1920s. In 1296 William de Kethkert appears on the "Ragman Roll", the document signed by those swearing allegiance to Edward I at the time of his invasion of Scotland. His successor, Sir Alan de Kethkert, however, is noted as a great friend of Robert the Bruce, whom he is said to have accompanied to the Crusades. By the mid fourteenth century the Cathcarts had also amassed extensive estates in Ayrshire. In 1447 James II elevated Sir Alan Cathcart to the title of Lord Cathcart and members of this important house were present at all the conflicts which shaped Scotland. Three sons of the house fell at Flodden (1513) and another at Pinkie (1547). From 1500 onwards the family fell on hard times and in 1543 or 1546 the third Earl sold his Renfrewshire estates. The largest part was sold to his wife's uncle Gabriel Semple and subsequently came into the hands of the Maxwells of Pollok. The tenth Lord Cathcart bought back the Cathcart portion of the estate in 1801 and was created an Earl in 1814.

In the north east corner of the parish lay the hamlet of Langside, a place which would have languished in utter obscurity had it not been for the decisive defeat of the forces of Mary, Queen of Scots here on 13 May 1568. By securing the higher ground and with superior leadership the armies of the Regent Moray repulsed a larger number of troops and ended the rule of Scotland by its last Catholic monarch. The meal mill of Langside features on a map of 1654 and was located on the Langside bank of the Cart on the west side of Millbrae. This remained a working mill, although certainly reconstructed, until it was destroyed by fire in 1848. A paper mill diagonally opposite operated briefly from c.1690 - 1729. The mansion of "Langsyid" is also noted in 1654. Through contracts of marriage and purchases most of the lands in the vicinity of Langside came into the possession of the Maxwells of Nether Pollok. Thomas Brown bought Langside in 1776 and it remained in the possession of his descendants until 1852. In 1777 Brown had Langside House rebuilt to a design by Robert Adam. This was demolished in the 1950s and the site has since been redeveloped as Langside Gardens.

Paper making was introduced to Cathcart in 1729 and in 1753 the road through the village was upgraded as part of a turnpike from the Gorbals to Carmunnock. By 1782 the village contained some thirty-six houses. In 1800, however, a new bridge was built downstream of the narrow span now known as the Snuff Mill Bridge. This was built to carry a new, superior road to Busby, now known as Clarkston Road, which was completed in 1810. With its construction, Cathcart was bypassed and its population diminished to just six or eight families, while a new village, New Cathcart, grew as a straggling ribbon development along the route of the new road.

In 1852 Neale Thomson, the owner of the lands of Camphill and Pathhead, which now form Queen's Park, bought the estate of Langside and immediately had feu plans drawn up for an extensive development of villas. However, only two of the feus were taken up, one by "Greek" Thomson's celebrated double villa (1856) and the other Rawcliffe House (1862). One reason for the failure of the plan was probably the absence of a reliable supply of piped fresh water. Glasgow's water began to be brought from Loch Katrine in 1868 and pipes were subsequently laid beyond the city boundary, which stimulated growth. Consequently Langside began to develop as a suburb of villas during the 1870s.

In 1890 Glasgow sought to expand the city boundaries to include many areas on the edges of the city which it had improved with road widening, gas and water supplies. Among the districts included in the Annexation Bill were Langside, its extension Battlefield, and the new suburb of Mount Florida. The citizens of Langside were convinced of the merits of annexation, despite an anticipated rise in rates, but opposition from other areas around the city which had declared themselves burghs led to the defeat of the Bill early in 1890. In May 1890 Mount Florida residents expressed the desire that a burgh be formed of their district,Langside, Shawlands and Crossmyloof. Langside, meanwhile sought independent burgh status on its own. However, common sense prevailed and on 1 November 1891 all were united with Glasgow, as were other areas on all sides of the city. Tenements began to fill up all the vacant ground in Langside and Battlefield during the 1890s and eventually surrounded Cathcart, itself annexed to Glasgow in 1912.

Today, the area covered by this book is largely intact and happily I have had to look for fewer synonyms for "demolished, knocked down, gubbed etc." than with other districts of the city. A few churches have gone, and modest mansions and villas have been casualties from the 1920s through to the 1970s. Three streets of 1870s villas in Langside were obliterated when barely a century old and replaced by modern flats, a reminder that large houses with grounds are cheaper to redevelop than densely populated rows of tenements. In general, however, Langside, Mount Florida and Cathcart form the most intact Victorian and Edwardian tenement district on the south side of Glasgow.

Eric Eunson, October 1999.

Old Houses at Battlefield, Langside, Glasgow

When the contactor William Waddell built the first tenements in Algie Place in 1895, one commentator remarked that the last of the old village, which stood opposite, must soon be erased. However, these eighteenth century buildings did survive for another decade and appear on several Edwardian postcards. The thatched cottage in the middle was even re-roofed in slate before 1905, but demolished soon after. In 1841 there were twenty-four households inLangside, most of whom were weavers, but the industry died out over the next thirty years as the proliferation of large textile mills ended the viability of the cottage industry throughout Scotland.

A Free Church congregation was formed in Langside in 1883 and worshipped first in a mission hall within the Camphill grounds. This soon proved inadequate and the trustees of Neale Thomson offered them a site for a larger church in 1894. This was an old property known as Queen Mary Cottage, which stood in its own grounds. The architect chosen to draw up plans was Alexander Skirving, then resident in the district. The foundation stone was laid on 21 September 1895 and the church opened on 5 November 1896. Skirving had been the chief draughtsman to Alexander "Greek" Thomson and the influence of his one time master is obvious in the Graeco Roman design. The church was closed in 1979 and by the late 1980s it was in a sorry state, its windows broken and rosebay sprouting from the roof. A subsequent fire looked to have sealed its fate, but it has since been refurbished as a bar and restaurant.

43090 JV

Collectors would give a fortune today for the advertising posters in this 1904 view of the Battlefield Monument - especially the one of the R.M.S. Columba. The monument stands on the site of a row of thatched cottages which were known as the "Cruikit Raw". On the right is the early nineteenth century Middlebank House, now the oldest building in Langside. In the 1860s it housed refreshment rooms and then the carriage hire and undertaking business of John Shand, established in 1875. The large villa among the trees was Overdale House, built for Robert Cochran c. 1870-75. It was bought by Glasgow Corporation in 1923, who built the electricity sub-station facing Battlefield Road in the grounds. The house itself was replaced by the modernist Lighting Department building in 1937-39.

Langside Parish Church was designed by Alexander Skirving in 1886 and replaced a temporary building in Blairhall Avenue, opened a decade earlier. Completed in 1888, it closed in the 1970s and was used by the Victoria Infirmary as a repository for records, among them a large quantity of highly combustable x-ray transparencies. In 1982 it was destroyed in a blaze which illuminated the night sky all over the south side. Skirving also designed the Battlefield Monument, erected by public subscription in 1888 when it was felt that a memorial to the battle should be put up before the advancing city obliterated all traces of the field. Under the column were placed newspapers and coins of the day and a copy of William Scott's recently published definitive history of the battle.

Millbrae Road looking north in 1904, showing part of Queen Mary Terrace on the right and Langside Place on the left. Langside sub-post office, just out of shot, is still in the same premises it occupied when opened in 1892. Millbrae Road follows the course of an old thoroughfare known as "The Vennel". Behind the south side of Langside Place stood Burnstyle farmhouse, demolished in the 1950s to make way for the Victoria Infirmary's Geriatric Unit. The telegram boy standing in the middle of the road would be taking his life in his hands nowadays. If you want to cross this busy arterial road in the rush hour, make sure you've got a spare thirty minutes!

OVERDALE VILLAS LANGESIDE

These villas in Overdale Street were built in 1893, when they were styled Landore Terrace. They were the last villas to be erected in Battlefield and subsequent developments consisted entirely of red sandstone tenements. In 1987 Richard Stenlake opened Glasgow's first shop devoted entirely to antique picture postcards and other paper collectables at No. 1 Overdale Street, ably assisted by Anthony Duda and myself. In February the following year Stenlake Publishing was launched with a modest little booklet of old pictures of Motherwell. I will always harbour happy memories of the Overdale Street shop, which closed in 1993, even if it was an oven in summer and a deep freeze in winter.

RAWCLIFFE HOUSE, LANGSIDE.

Rawcliffe Lodge was built in 1861-62 for Alexander Stewart of the firm Stewart & MacDonald, whose extensive premises occupied the building now occupied by Fraser's store on the corner of Argyle Street and Buchanan Street. By 1900 they had two extensive facories in Glasgow, one making mantles and underclothing, the other shirts and slops, and had retail warehouses in Leeds and London. The lodge was designed to resemble a French chateau, a style made briefly popular by the building of Balmoral Castle in 1853. In 1919 Rawcliffe became a monastery of Carmelite nuns (contrary to popular belief, the word monastery can be applied to religious houses of either gender).

Millbrae Crescent, Langside, Glasgow

Leafy Millbrae Crescent has hardly changed since this 1907 postcard was published. The two storey terrace is believed to be the work of Robert Turnbull and was built in 1875. Turnbull was the partner of the celebrated Alexander "Greek" Thomson who died in the same year and his influence is evident here, with lotus columns flanking the entrances and capping the chimneys among the Neo-Classical details. The tenements on the other side of the street were built in 1893.

SINCLAIR DRIVE, LANGSIDE

The first tenements in Sinclair Drive were erected in 1893 and this view of the completed street, with the junction with Overdale Street on the right, was published c.1910. Sinclair Drive is named after Alexander Sinclair, a prominent Battlefield citizen of the late nineteenth century who lived at Ajmere in Cathkin Road. He began working for the Glasgow Herald in 1845 at the age of sixteen, where he had the humble job of addressing bundles of newspapers. He worked his way up, eventually becoming manager, a position he held for fifty years.

Sinclair Drive from Ledard Road in 1910, looking toward the River Cart. Colleagues remembered Alex Sinclair as "aquiline and handsomely bearded" and a serious man who seldom smiled. He was one of the chief promoters of the erection of the Battlefield Monument and was instrumental in persuading the people of Langside to accept annexation by the City of Glasgow in 1891.

The Boys' Brigade are marching past Battlefield West Church in Ledard Road in this 1920s view. The church was built in 1909 to provide additional Established Church accomodation after Langside Old Parish Church beside the Victoria Infirmary had become insufficient for the needs of the growing suburb. The architect Henry E. Clifford drew his inspiration for the design from Dunblane Cathedral. In the early 1990s the building was found to be riddled with dry rot and the elders and congregation arrived at the painful decision that the only solution was to demolish it and build a completely new church, completed in 1996.

LOCHLEVEN . ROAD   (469)

Lochleven Street, built in 1900-01, recalls Queen Mary's incarceration in the island fortress of Loch Leven in 1567, following the Battle of Carberry. This was caused by Mary's alleged complicity in the murder of her husband, Henry Lord Darnley, and subsequent remarriage to the ambitious Bothwell. Her escape with the aid of the young boatman Willie Douglas is one of the most famous episodes in her life. This took place on 2 May 1568; the Battle of Langside was fought eleven days later. This 1910 view is the work of Willie Ross whose studio was located at 23 Paterson Street, Tradeston. He was the most prolific Edwardian photographer of south side street scenes, but individually his views are all rare and eagerly sought.

The nucleus of Queen's Park School was formed in Strathbungo in 1873 and transferred to a new building in Grange Road in 1874, which was soon extended. The building in this 1908 view was built as a higher grade secondary school in 1900-02 and was designed by H. & D. Barclay. A replacement for the primary school was begun in 1912 but never completed owing to the outbreak of war. Between 1907 and 1912 all the primary pupils were transferred to a new school in Cuthbertson Street and the three Queen's Park buildings became one higher grade school. The secondary school closed in 1994 and became a teachers' resource centre. The 1902 building illustrated was destroyed by fire the following year.

Victoria Infirmary, Glasgow.

The building of the Victoria Infirmary was partly funded by bequests of £10,000 from William Dixon of the Govan Iron works and £40,000 from William Couper of Millholm Paper Mill. The original design was by James Sellars and construction began in 1888. Following his death the same year, its completion was overseen by his partner John Campbell. The Grange Road facade in this 1922 picture was obscured by the erection of what was then a private patients' wing, built in 1931 and extended in 1935. The Battlefield Rest was designed by Burnet and Boston in 1914-15 and contained a shelter, lavatories and news stand for the convenience of tram passengers. After facing a very uncertain future for many years this unique building has recently been converted into a restaurant.

Kitchen staff at the Victoria in 1907. The sender of the postcard says that the man on the right of the picture is the cook and adds, with a political incorrectness common for the time, "we are a lot of coolies". The nurses' home to the north of the hospital was built in 1928-30 and extended in 1937. The hospital itself was extensively enlarged on the Grange Road side throughout the 1960s. In recent years the "Vicky" has seen its acute services whittled down as departments are relocated to the "Sufferin' General". This has meant services being removed from a central location, well served by public transport, to a remote and inaccessible hospital on the margin of the city. Surely the under used and waterlogged Queen's Park recreation grounds would make an ideal site for the expansion of this valuable hospital?

The Deaf and Dumb Institution in Prospecthill Road opened in 1868 and replaced an earlier city centre institution in Parson Street. The architect of this Gothic pile was James Salmon senior. Closed during World War II, the building reopened in 1947 as Langside College. Between 1958 and 1965 extensive additions were made by Boussevain and Osmond. This illustration of the original building dates from 1897.

Founded in 1867, Queen's Park F.C. is the oldest league club in Scotland. For the first six years of its existence the club played its home matches on the Queen's Park Recreation Ground, before moving to a custom built stadium in 1873. This was named Hampden Park after Hampden Place, a newly built terrace in Mount Florida. When they vacated the ground in favour of the site of the present Hampden Park in 1903, it was taken over by Third Lanark F.C. who renamed it Cathkin Park. Formed in 1872 Third Lanark were relegated to the second division in 1965 and folded in 1967, amid claims that one man, William Hiddleston, had acquired a controlling interest in the club with a view to winding it up and selling off its assets. This view of Cathkin Park, then Hampden, was taken in 1895. The absence of Myrtle Park in Crosshill makes the Dixon Halls appear deceptively close.

The first part of the Cathcart District Railway was opened from Pollokshields East to Mount Florida on 1 March 1886, with additional stations at Queen's Park and Crosshill. On 25 May 1886 it was completed as far as Cathcart. It was run as a branch from Glasgow Central and in 1887 the company got permission to complete the circle back to the city via Langside, Shawlands, Maxwell Park and Pollokshields West. In 1887 eighty-nine trains a day ran on the Cathcart Circle and the busy commuter line stimulated the development of all the districts it served, not least the embryonic Mount Florida which entered its peak period of growth. This view of the much altered station dates from 1907.

The first horse-drawn trams in Glasgow were introduced by a private company in 1872 and by the time the Corporation took over the service in 1880 the lines stretched to Mount Florida. Although the services were extended to Cathcart in 1902, the same year the whole system was electrified, Mount Florida remained the terminus for three of the city's main tram routes. Hampden Place, the first block to be completed on this stretch of Cathcart Road in 1873, can just be glimpsed on the left of this 1907 view. Its neighbour, the distinctly Parisienne Lorne Place, was built in 1878

Cathcart Road, Mount Florida.

Mount Florida, literally meaning "mount abounding in flowers", began as a suburb of prestigious terraced villas, such as those in Stanmore Road, in the 1870s. Development here and throughout the city halted abruptly with the collapse of the City of Glasgow Bank in 1878, which brought ruin to builders and financiers. When building resumed in Mount Florida in the 1880s subsequent development of the area consisted of four storey tenements aimed at blue collar workers. This vista looking back toward the city was posted in 1915.

Cathcart Road, Mount Florida

This superb view dates from the late 1920s. The shop on the corner of the domed tenement is a branch of R.S. McColl. "Sweetie" McColl was a famous Queen's Park player and was considered in his day to be the finest centreforward the team had ever had. He retired from league football in 1910, when he hammered home six goals for the "Spiders" in a match against Port Glasgow. He opened his first confectioner's shop at 78 New City Road in 1905 and by the 1930s the chain which bore his name had more than sixty shops across the city.

Carmunnock Road, Mount Florida

Mount Florida Primary School, just visible on the right, was built in 1895. The Art Nouveau inspired tenement opposite was completed in 1909. The old road from the Gorbals via Cathcart to Carmunnock was upgraded into a turnpike in 1753 and as it linked up with other routes to the south became a vital artery into the city. The woods of Linn Park are just visible in the background of this atmospheric 1920s view.

The third Hampden Park opened in 1903 and was designed by Archibald Leitch, who also designed Ibrox and Celtic Park. The east and west stands and pavilion were destroyed by fire in 1905 and the replacement east stand, completed in 1908, can be seen on the right of this 1910 view. Scotland won this April 2 clash with the "Auld Enemy" 2-0, but I wonder how many fans on either side were aware that Hampden Place, after which the ground was named, was itself named after John Hampden (1594-1643) an English Parliamentarian and hero of the Civil War. By an arbitrary quirk of fate the flagship of Scottish Anglophobia is named after an Englishman!

The wooden stands in the previous view were replaced in 1914 by the brick buildings visible in this late 1930s picture. The photograph was taken from Kingsacre Road, King's Park. The completion of a new north stand in 1937 increased ground capacity to 150,000, making Hampden the largest stadium in the world, a record superceded in 1950 with the completion of the Maracana Stadium in Brazil. By the 1960s the ill-maintained ground had become a national disgrace and there were calls for it to be rebuilt. However, it was not until 1981 that its redevelopment began with the rebuilding of the east stand. In the wake of the Bradford and Hillsborough disasters strict new regulations were introduced and a major reconstruction of the whole stadium began in 1995.

HOLMLEA ALLOTMENTS

EFFECTS OF THE FLOOD 18/8/20

The drowned allotments in this picture were replaced in the 1930s by the Holmlea Recreation Grounds. The White Cart rises above Eaglesham, flows through Cathcart and, joining the Black Cart at Inchinnan, flows into the Clyde opposite Clydebank. Glasgow District Council dredged the Cart to prevent flooding into the 1970s, when this was abandoned in favour of a scheme to tame the river by enclosing stretches of it within dykes. However, when these were breached several times the effect was that of a dam bursting and the force of the floodwater caused considerable damage to property. A pressure group of locals are presently continuing a long battle to have the dredging of the Cart resumed.

HOLMLEA RD FROM NEW BRIDGE.

The new Holmlea Bridge across the Cart was completed in 1901 to enable Glasgow's tramways to be extended to Netherlee. It replaced an old span known as the Hunchback Bridge, which dated from 1800. The new bridge stimulated the development of tenement building and within two years most of Holmlea Road had been built up. Holmlea Primary School on the left of this 1910 picture was built in 1908.

Wallace Scott Tailoring Institue, Cathcart.

The Wallace-Scott Tailoring Institute was designed by Sir. J.J. Burnett, begun in 1913 and completed in 1922. It was a model factory and its workers were provided with gardens, tennis courts, a bowling green and sports ground. By the 1940s the company slogan was "Honest endeavour, loyal teamwork, a deaf ear turned to every whisper of self-satisfaction, these are the needle, thread and chalk at Cathcart". The building became the headquarters of the South of Scotland Electricity Board in the early 1950s. Its architecture has since been given a makeover of bland modernity and its pleasure grounds have vanished under extensions and car parks.

HOLMHEAD CRESENT. CATHCART.

Holmhead Crescent, Street, Terrace and Place were built on the site of Geddes' Dyeworks and Carpet Factory. The firm prospered around the middle of the nineteenth century, but closed in the 1880s after a period of decline. Part of George and James Weir's works occupy the foreground of this 1905 view. Weirs' was established in Cathcart in 1886 and specialised in marine engineering. During the 1914-18 war the firm diversified into making shells, gun carriages and aeroplane components, and during the 1930s carried out pioneering work on auto-gyro's and helicopters. Now trading as Weir Pumps Ltd., the company still prospers making marine, power station, oil industry, condensing and desalination plant.

The site of Cathcart's original church has been lost, but it is presumed to have been somewhere in the kirkyard of its eighteenth and nineteenth century successors. A new church was erected in 1707 and was remodelled in 1744. However, by 1828 this had become dilapidated and the Gothic church in this 1904 picture was completed in 1831. The architect was James Dempster and he repeated the design at Mauchline and Cardross. The body of the kirk was demolished in 1931, leaving only the tower. The church bell continued to be rung from here until 1958, when it was transferred to the present church for safety reasons.

Raising the roof - literally - during the construction of the replacement Old Cathcart Parish Church in 1929. The contractors were Dewar and Elliot of Pollokshaws Road, Govanhill. More construction is going on in the background beyond the Cathcart Junction railway embankment as work continues on McTaggart and Mickel's new suburb of King's Park, begun in 1925. The field between the chuch and the railway is now filled with inter-war housing.

H.E. Clifford drew up plans for the new church in 1914, but the building had just begun when it had be halted owing to the war. It was not restarted until 1923 when Watson, Salmond and Gray were the architects employed to oversee the completion of the work. The foundation stone was laid on 25 March 1928 by Lord Tweedsmuir, better known as the author John Buchan. It is worth noting that the foundation stone is not necessarily the first stone of a building, nor is it generally part of the foundations!

Despite the erection of late nineteenth century tenements and villas, Cathcart still retained much of the character of a rural Renfrewshire village when this 1905 postcard of Old Castle Road was published. The building in the right foreground was the village blacksmith's shop, occupied for generations by the Peddie family. It is said that Rabbie Burns once had his horse shod here. In the late nineteenth century Robert Peddie established an infirmary for dogs on the first floor and part of the sign can be seen on the gable of the building. The smithy fell derelict in the 1960s and was damaged by fire. However, it was refurbished in the mid 1970s as a licensed restaurant.

A turn of the century view of Old Castle Road with the entrance to Snuffmill Road at the end of the street. The seventeenth century thatched cottages were probably the homes of workers at the nearby meal mill, later paper mill. Picturesque but primitive, they were pulled down before 1914. The site was occupied during the last war by prefabs but these in turn gave way to council houses in the 1960s.

This Old Cathcart hostelry stood in Snuffmill Road and was known as "The Wee Thack Hoose in the Glen" and latterly Granny Robertson's, after its last proprietrix, Jane Robertson. The building was three centuries old when it was condemned in 1893. Its licence was transferred to a shop at the corner of Old Castle Road and Crompton Avenue, which continued as "Ye Old Hoose" until Cathcart voted "dry" in 1920. There were four pubs in Cathcart at that time and all were forced to close. Plebiscites were taken in 1926 and 1965, but the vote was still for "no change". The liquor licence granted to the Old Smiddy restaurant in the mid 1970s was the first in Cathcart for more than fifty years.

Old Bridge and Snuff Mill, Cathcart.

43093, JV.

In 1812 Solomon Lindsay bought the eighteenth century meal mill on the Cart and converted it into a paper mill. Its main product was cardboard used in bookbinding, but in 1814 a small part of the mill was let to James Hartley who used it for the manufacture of snuff. Solomon Lindsay died in 1859 and his son carried on the business until 1902. The old cottage he occupied was demolished three years later and Mill House erected in its stead. The building on the left of this Edwardian view is dated 1858. 39

There is some debate about the true age of the Snuff Mill Bridge, which bears a datestone of 1624. However, examination of its neat ashlar construction can leave little doubt that this stone has been inserted into an eighteenth century reconstruction, possibly contemporary with the Gorbals-Carmunnock turnpike of 1753. The house on the left of this 1905 view was built for the paper maker David Lindsay in 1863-64, in anticipation of his forthcoming marriage. The house was designed by John Baird II and has a monogram over the main entrance incorporating all the letters of the name Lindsay. The fireplace openings on the gable suggest that it was anticipated to be the first of a terrace of houses. Lindsay, however, did not prosper and soon moved back to the old mill cottage and his villa became a tenement.

A delightful study of Castle Road dated 1904, which the sender has titled "The Never Never Land"

This stone marks the point from which Mary is supposed to have viewed her defeat at Langside. The spot was long marked by a thorn bush and when this died off around 1799, General Sir George Cathcart erected a rough hewn stone carved by his own hand with a crown and "M.R., 1568". The present stone was erected by his nephew in the late nineteenth century. There is some doubt as to whether Mary actually viewed the battle from this spot, just yards from the castle of Sir William Semple who was fighting on the opposite side. The highest point of the Cathkin Braes is also claimed as the spot from which Mary observed her defeat.

41

Although it probably contained elements of an earlier building, Cathcart Castle was essentially a typical sixteenth century Scottish tower house. When entire it had five storeys and was surrounded by a "barmkin", a battlemented wall with turrets at the angles. The interior was remodelled in brick rendered with decorated plaster in the seventeenth century. It was abandoned as a place of residence around 1740. Tradition maintains it was bought by a builder intent on treating it as a quarry, who found it too well built to demolish. No such problem troubled Glasgow District Council who pronounced it unsafe and tore it down without warning or consultation in 1980. The cottages on the right of this 1911 view were removed in the 1920s.

When the Cathcart estate was broken up in the eighteenth century the portion containing the disused castle was bought by James Hill, a Glasgow lawyer. Around 1780 he built Cathcart House, a short distance to the east of the castle, which satisfied the contemporary fashion for having a picturesque ruin in the vicinity of a country seat. In 1801 the Earl of Cathcart bought back the estate and mansion. It was variously inhabited by members of the Cathcart family and sometimes let to Glasgow's nouveau riche. The mansion was demolished in 1927 when its lands were bought by the Corporation and united with Linn Park.

ILLHOLM PAPER MILL. CATHCART

STARK SERIES. REG

The Millholm Paper Mill was begun in 1729 by Nicholas Deschamp and was a successor to a paper mill he had founded at Langside c.1690. He had arrived in Scotland shortly before this date as a Hugenot refugee fleeing persecution in his native France. His daughter married J. Hall and the Halls owned Millholm until 1800. In 1853 it was sold to Robert and James Couper, tenants since 1841. It was sold again in 1884 and passed through a number of hands before becoming part of the Wiggins Teape organisation. It was closed in the 1920s and partly demolished in 1938. The building on the right of this 1903 view was converted into an engineering works in 1947 and gutted by fire in 1953.

The Waterfall,
Linn Estate, Cathcart

The upper part of Linn Park was acquired by the Corporation in 1919 and comprised the early nineteenth century Linn House and its policies, including the Linn or waterfall after which it is named and the Halfpenny Bridge. This dates from c.1835 and is the oldest iron bridge in the city. Its name is thought to derive from the numerous circles in its design, for it was certainly never a toll bridge. The Cathcart end, including Cathcart House, was added in 1927 and Court Knowe in 1933. The Linn Sawmill in this early 1920s view was in the hands of David Allan by 1875 and he was still there in 1911 although it disappears from directories after this date. It was demolished in 1927 during the laying out of the park.

When the Corporation acquired the first part of Linn Park they opened the former Linn Mansion as a tearoom in 1921. A second tearoom was opened at the Netherlee end of the park c.1930. The Tower De Paris (the French is wrong, it should have been "Tour"!) was built in the fashionable Art Deco style, but its outwardly solid appearance concealed the fact that it was really little more than a big wooden shed.

Inter-war elegance inside the Tower De Paris Tearooms, where tea, coffee, ice cream sodas, freshly baked cakes, hot pies and a vast array of confectionery could be enjoyed amid surroundings of chromed cake stands, starched linen table cloths and potted palms. The tearoom has long since gone, but its site was in the vicinity of McLaren Place. Although Glasgow has more green spaces than any other city in Europe, hence the epithet the "Dear Green Place", many of the city's parks are little used. Linn Park is one of these, a pity since it is one of the most beautiful areas of natural woodland in the city. A visit is strongly recommended, but if you want a cup of tea today you'll have to bring a Thermos.

The "dead centre" of Cathcart on a 1904 picture postcard (wish you were here?). The cemetery in Benfield Road was laid out according to plans by W.R. McKelvie of Dundee and opened in 1878. Wooded cemeteries are very uncommon in Scotland and the tree roots have tilted many of the stones to weird angles. It is simultaneously picturesque and spooky!

48